I0440883

Wetlands of International Importance

"The Mission of the U.S. Fish and Wildlife Service is working with others to conserve, protect and enhance fish, wildlife, plants and their habitats for the continuing benefit of the American people."

Cover:
Scenic wetland
USFWS

What is the Convention on Wetlands of International Importance?

The Convention on Wetlands of International Importance especially as Waterfowl Habitat—also known as the Ramsar Convention on Wetlands from its place of adoption in 1971 in Iran—is an intergovernmental treaty that provides a framework for international cooperation for the conservation of wetland habitats.

The major objectives of the Convention are to stem the loss of wetlands and to ensure their conservation. To meet these objectives, the Convention places general obligations on its member countries, or Contracting Parties, relating to the conservation of wetlands within their boundaries, and special obligations pertaining to those wetlands which have been designated in a "List of Wetlands of International Importance."

> *The major objectives of the Convention are to stem the loss of wetlands and to ensure their conservation.*

The Convention went into effect in 1975, after the accession of its seventh country, Greece. The United States became a member in 1986, when the U.S. Senate ratified and the President signed the Instruments of Ratification. The U.S. Fish and Wildlife Service and the U.S. Department of State are responsible for implementation of the Convention in the United States. More than 122 countries, from all regions of the world, are now Contracting Parties to the Convention.

What areas can be covered by the Convention?

Just as in the United States, the word "wetlands" encompasses a wide variety of habitats around the world. The Convention takes a very broad approach in determining which wetlands may come under its aegis. The Convention considers wetlands as "areas of marsh, fen, peatland or water, whether natural or artificial, permanent or temporary, with water that is static or flowing, fresh, brackish

...the Convention extends to a wide variety of habitat types including rivers, coastal areas and even coral reefs.

or salt, including areas of marine water, the depth of which at low tide does not exceed six meters." Additionally, the Convention provides that wetlands "may incorporate riparian and coastal zones adjacent to the wetlands, and islands or bodies of marine water deeper than six meters at low tide lying within the wetlands." As a result of these provisions, the coverage of the Convention extends to a wide variety of habitat types including rivers, coastal areas and even coral reefs.

Above:
Mountain Marsh
USFWS
Opposite page:
Coral Reef
USFWS/Gil Cintron

Why conserve wetlands?

Wetlands are among the most productive environments in the United States, and in the world. They provide economic benefits through fish and shellfish production (over two thirds of the world's fish harvest is linked to the health of wetland areas); the maintenance of water tables for agriculture; water storage and flood control; shoreline stabilization; hay and silage production; water purification; and recreational opportunities.

The Convention's official name includes the phrase "...especially as Waterfowl Habitat." The United States has long recognized the great value of wetlands to waterfowl, as well as to other migratory birds. The nation's very first national wildlife refuge, created by President Theodore Roosevelt in 1903, was a wetland—Pelican Island, a three-acre nesting and rookery island in Florida's Indian River. In 1918 the U.S. passed into law the Migratory Bird Treaty Act, ratifying a treaty with Great Britain, on behalf of Canada, that recognized the conservation responsibilities for the more than 800 species of migratory birds shared by the two countries. As an outgrowth of that act, and subsequent conservation laws and treaties, the United States developed a system of 525 national wildlife refuges, totaling more than 93 million acres. Many of these refuges are strategically located complexes of wetlands designed to protect and conserve nesting, resting and wintering sites for waterfowl and migratory shore and wading birds.

Wetlands also provide habitat for countless species of mammals, reptiles, amphibians, fish and invertebrates, as well as an amazing variety of plant life. Though the United States lost more than half its original wetlands during the period from the 1780's to the 1980's, the remaining 100+ million acres of wetlands provide some of this nation's greatest examples of biological diversity, as well as vital habitat to many listed species of threatened and endangered plants and animals.

Obligations under the Convention

The Convention is *not* an international regulatory mechanism, nor does it presume to impose any restrictions or conditions that affect in any way the sovereignty of countries.

Under the Convention there is a general obligation for member countries to include wetland conservation considerations in their natural resources planning processes (if they have such processes), and to promote the wise use of wetlands within their territory. This wise use requirement is understood to mean maintenance of the ecological character of wetlands, which defines the site's functional values.

> *...promote the conservation of wetlands ...through the establishment of nature reserves.*

A second obligation under the Convention is the designation of wetlands for inclusion in a "List of Wetlands of International Importance." At least one site must be designated by each member country, with selection based on "international significance" in terms of ecology, botany, zoology, limnology or hydrology. Criteria for identifying and duties for conserving wetlands of international importance have been adopted by countries under the Convention.

Lastly, countries are obliged to promote the conservation of wetlands in their territory (whether or not the wetlands are included on the List) through the establishment of nature reserves.

Opposite page:
Coastal mudflats in Panama
Ramsar Secretariat

How does the Convention operate?

Member countries meet every three years to discuss progress in wetlands conservation, to review the status of sites on the List, to hear reports from international organizations and to make decisions on the functioning of the Convention. The Convention has a financial management system, a Standing Committee and a Bureau or Secretariat. Member countries contribute annually to support the Convention. The Standing Committee—made up of representatives from nine member countries—carries out the interim activities between conferences. (The United States served as Chair of the Standing Committee from 1990-93.) The

The Convention has a financial management system, a Standing Committee and a Bureau or Secretariat.

independent Ramsar Bureau, located in Gland, Switzerland, also works in cooperation with four partner non-governmental organizations (NGOs): BirdLife International, The World Conservation Union (IUCN), Wetlands International, and World Wide Fund for Nature International (WWF). Other NGOs may become partners to the Convention. The Bureau provides a permanent structure for administrative, scientific and technical support.

The List of Wetlands of International Importance

Of all aspects of the Convention, the List has attracted the greatest international attention. Placing an area on the "Ramsar List" has had considerable impact upon the conservation of the area and upon public recognition of the global importance of the site.

To date the member countries have collectively designated 1,031 sites covering more than 193 million acres, and new sites are added regularly. Although most countries have designated wetland sites for the List on the basis of their importance for birds, fish and other wildlife, habitat characteristics are also taken into account, with the result that a rather comprehensive selection of major wetland types is included on the List.

Placing an area on the "Ramsar List" has had considerable impact upon the conservation of the area and upon public recognition of the global importance of the site.

Above:
Waterfall in Niger
Ramsar Secretariat
Opposite page:
Caddo Lake, Texas. Ramsar site listed in 1993.
USFWS

How do U.S. sites get selected for the List?

The Convention provides criteria for member countries to use in making their nominations for the Ramsar List. A wetland is suitable for inclusion in the List if it meets any *one* of these:

1. Criteria for representative or unique wetlands. A wetland should be considered internationally important if: a) it is a particularly good representative example of a natural or near-natural wetland, characteristic of the appropriate biogeographical region; or b) it is a particularly good representative example of a natural or near-natural wetland, common to more than one biogeographical region; or c) it is a particularly good representative example of a wetland which plays a substantial hydrological, biological or ecological role in the natural

Above:
Salamander
Ramsar Secretariat
Opposite page:
Bottomland hardwood
USFWS/Bob Misso

functioning of a major river basin or coastal system, especially where it is located in a transborder position; or d) it is an example of a specific type of wetland, rare or unusual in the appropriate biogeographical region.

2. General criteria based on plants or animals. A wetland should be considered internationally important if: a) it supports an appreciable assemblage of rare, vulnerable or endangered species or subspecies of plant or animal, or an appreciable number of individuals of any one or more of these species; or b) it is of special value for maintaining the genetic and ecological diversity of a region because of the quality and peculiarities of its flora and fauna; or c) it is of special value as the habitat of plants or animals at a critical stage of their biological cycle; or d) it is of special value for one or more endemic plant or animal species or communities.

3. Criteria based on waterfowl. A wetland should be considered internationally important if: a) it regularly supports 20,000 waterfowl; or b) it regularly supports substantial numbers of individuals from particular groups of waterfowl, indicative of wetland values, productivity or diversity; or c) where data on popula-

tions are available, it regularly supports 1% of the individuals in a population of one species or subspecies of waterfowl.

(NB: The use of the term waterfowl refers to all water birds, including ducks, geese, shorebirds, wading birds, and sea birds).

4. Criteria based on fish. A wetland should be considered internationally important if: a) it supports a significant proportion of indigenous fish subspecies, species or families, life-history stages, species interactions and/or populations that are representative of wetland benefits and/or values and thereby contributes to global biological diversity; or b) it is an important source of food for fishes, spawning ground, nursery and/or migration path on which fish stocks, either within the wetland or elsewhere, depend.

Above:
Yacara caiman
Ramsar Secretariat
Opposite page:
Waterlily and cypress
USFWS/Dan O'Neal

Wetlands and wise use

Inclusion of a site on the Ramsar List certainly does not preclude a wide array of wetland uses, so long as these are wise uses—uses that do not upset the biological, hydrological, and physical relationships critical to the functioning of the site. Wise use is encouraged.

The Ramsar Convention defines wise use of wetlands as "their sustainable utilization for the benefit of humankind in a way compatible with the maintenance of the natural properties of the ecosystem." Sustainable utilization is the human use of a wetland so that it may yield the greatest continuous benefit to present generations while maintaining its potential to meet the needs and aspirations of future generations.

Above:
Bond Swamp National Wildlife Refuge, Georgia
USFWS/Hollingsworth
Opposite page:
Wise use
USFWS/Robert J. Bridges

Procedures for selecting U.S. wetlands for the List

Just about any local government, group, community, or private organization in the United States can nominate a site for inclusion on the Ramsar List. This is provided the area in question meets the Ramsar criteria for inclusion and that the site's landowners and various stakeholders agree to its inclusion. In addition, state and federal agencies can make nominations.

The procedure for nomination involves submitting a letter and a map to the Director, U.S. Fish and Wildlife Service, describing how the proposed site meets the criteria and indicating its location (using longitude and latitude). The nomination must also have a completed *Information Sheet on Ramsar Wetlands* (obtainable from the address below or from the Ramsar web site: www.ramsar.org), and letters of concurrence from the wildlife or natural resources agency and member of Congress for the State in which the site is located. Organizations wishing to petition for listing a site under the Convention are invited to contact the U.S. Fish and Wildlife Service's Division of International Conservation at 4401 N. Fairfax Drive, Suite 730, Arlington, VA 22203-1622.

Right:
Sand Lake National Wildlife Refuge site designation in 1998
USFWS
Opposite page:
Izembek National Wildlife Refuge. Ramsar site listed in 1987
USFWS/John Sarvis